SMALL

WARS

MANUAL

Also by Chris Santiago

Tula

SMALL

WARS

MANUAL

poems

CHRIS SANTIAGO

MILKWEED EDITIONS

Published 2025 by Milkweed Editions
Printed in Canada
Cover design by Mary Austin Speaker
Cover photo by David Levinthal
Author photo by Mark Brown
25 26 27 28 29   5 4 3 2 1
First Edition

Library of Congress Cataloging-in-Publication Data

Names: Santiago, Chris, author.
Title: Small wars manual : poems / Christopher Santiago.
Description: First edition. | Minneapolis : Milkweed Editions, 2025. |
    Summary: "A far-reaching collection of erasures and original poems
    examining the long shadow of American militarism and imperialism"--
    Provided by publisher.
Identifiers: LCCN 2024049514 (print) | LCCN 2024049515 (ebook) |
    ISBN 9781571315717 (paperback) | ISBN 9781571317971 (ebook)
Subjects: LCGFT: Poetry.
Classification: LCC PS3619.A573 S63 2025 (print) | LCC PS3619.A573
    (ebook) | DDC 811/.6--dc23/eng/20241024
LC record available at https://lccn.loc.gov/2024049514
LC ebook record available at https://lccn.loc.gov/2024049515

Milkweed Editions is committed to ecological stewardship. We strive to align our book production practices with this principle, and to reduce the impact of our operations in the environment. We are a member of the Green Press Initiative, a nonprofit coalition of publishers, manufacturers, and authors working to protect the world's endangered forests and conserve natural resources. *Small Wars Manual* was printed on acid-free 100% postconsumer-waste paper by Friesens Corporation.

For Yuri, Aki & Tristan

Contents

Plate 1 — Regions of the horse and mule

Supply

Organization of a Constabulary

Plate 2 — Bones and joints of the horse and mule

Personnel

Diagram of a Message Pick-up

Erasure became like a form of reading, or detection. Which made me feel, as I do now, that writing itself is a form of reading.

—Srikanth Reddy, "The Weight of What's Left [Out]"

SMALL

WARS

MANUAL

2.1

(Organization: The estimate of the situation)

Note: The poems with numbered titles (including this one) form a series that erases the United States Marine Corps *Small Wars Manual.*

Methods: Each poem in this series has been "salvaged" from a single section or chapter of the *Manual.* In some cases, words have been assembled from the letters or fragments of other words. For example: *inter-* in *intervention* plus *-red* in *considered* becomes *interred.*

Typography: Punctuation and capitalization have been added for clarity. With a few exceptions, unused letters and spaces have been removed.

Restricted

3.1

(Logistics: Introduction)

3-1. Logistics is that branch of the military art which embraces the details of transportation and supplies.

"The Tables of Equipment, Supplies, and Tonnage, U. S. Marine Corps," set forth the equipment and supplies that are prescribed for Marine Corps expeditionary forces to take the field. These tables are a guide to the fourth section of the commander's executive staff in making a decision as to the type and amount of transportation and supplies required. However, the supply on hand at the port of embarkation, the time allowed for preparations, the ship's storage space available, the supplies in the theater of operations, the distance from home ports, when replacements can be expected on the foreign shore, and the condition of the roads and the road net within the anticipated field of operations will all be essential and controlling factors in arriving at the final decision.

```
                s              e        t

        The Table        p              a                    i
   r              the
                                                        gu
      e     s  t                  s   cut    a
      s         p                ra
              y                      of
   p e    on      i       e s
      f o   r     the    ce              n        t
 e                    r
              p   ie
 c                        e
```

Set the table, pair the guests—

cut a spray

         of peonies

               for the centerpiece—

5.3

(Initial Operations: Military territorial organization)

pyromancy   divination through fire

macharomancy   divination with daggers and swords

extispicy   interprets the remains of sacrificed animals

nggàm   the unrest of spiders and crabs

skatharomancers   observe the rooting of beetles over the graves
        of the murdered

5.4

stichomancy   uses poetry to tell the future

                                    from *stikhos*   Greek

                                    for lines of verse

                                    e.g. the Sortes Virgilianae

                                    prophecy through the writings of Virgil

                                    books chopped

                                    carved into wooden lots

                                    then dropped into urns

                                    and drawn at random

out of fragments one could learn

the doom of a house

or even a nation

6.5

(Infantry Patrols: The march)

Dawn in a shit-
hole country

the trails tortuous
minds immutable.

A day's march into
hostile terrain (mountainous,

heavily wooded) the patrol
is cut down to three:

an officer. A cook.
A native interpreter.

They pass in silence
over vast distances, homesick,

strangely disguised, stopping
only to gamble or drink.

The native takes the first watch.

Nightmares he mutters
are local weather: Men

should not sleep well on ground
tilled with lashings and hangings.

2.2

(Organization: The staff in small wars)

The surgeon	performs surgical strikes
The special staff	drown / out the sound of lids / and typewriters
The force commander	will accept *tactical pause* but not *ceasefire*
Drone operators	unacknowledged legislators of the world
The military governor	See *Taft, William Howard.*
Friendly natives	lost / in thought / lost in postprandial musings
The communications officer	████████████████████
The Bureau of Enemy Information	Daniel 2:4—Tell your servants the dream; we will interpret it.
The photographer	makes men / out of toy brigades / and vice versa

The speaker   bloodless //
                                 and impartial as / an unmanned //
                                 aerial vehicle

The "I"   See *Chapter IX: Aviation.*

The reader   See *above.* See *below.* See.

The civilians   [.]

1.2

(Introduction: Strategy)

one

a cadet

                    is

                    trained

to

     read

         the Rules of War

           but

      a

                commander in the

field

          is

    an

outlaw

a breach
in

the

subparagraph

two

a small war is a text

honeycombed with errata

three

camps

are the wages

of intervention

1.4

(Introduction: Relationship with the State Department)

they calculate parallax

cheek weld

scope shadow

adjust for cant

cosine indicators

recoil

watch for trace

and windage when

they were born to solve

                              the

                great

                machinery of

        nature

5.1

(Initial Operations: Neutral zones)

The origin of the world

is the building

of a border.

o

        If being

is a refuge

from nothingness

then war is the establishment

of a neutral zone.

o

Refugees

stream onto vessels

into asylum centers

unable to parse

the local language

o

or the difference

between the deported

and the departed.

6.6

(Infantry Patrols: Reconnaissance and security)

To uncover an enemy

in the field set the field

on fire   follow

the sound the

rapture follow

false maps

cities over-

run by feral dogs

keep the exit close

but keep your rifle

closer

14.5

(Supervision of Elections: Registration and voting)

The president from Canton

Ohio hears voices

hears angels

in the Oval Office encouraging

territorial expansion

one a fiery rooster   the other

a bull made of crude

                dip one finger

they hiss in the confluence

of Capital and Empire

but before he can fulfill

the vision the voices

abandon him in the Temple

of Music

1.1

(Introduction: General characteristics)

A "small war"

is a state of exception:

lawlessness

justified by the need to protect

property / and the lives

of propertied citizens.

The first phase is tropical

thirsty

for global markets;

the second involves steam-

ships and believers ex-

pedited to the Far East.

Martial law prepares the way

for the fourth phase:

erasure. Last

comes carabao skin

and mahajua wood for

the floors of the Oval Office.

4.3

(Training: Training en route on board ship)

Eighteen ninety-nine.

A colored private

quarrels with a white one; soon

everyone on board

is throwing hands.

It's a form of seasickness.

It's because home

is five-thousand miles away

and the physics of the Gilded Age

no longer apply.

        The sea is a country

that nullifies whiteness, every wave

that beats the ship

a separate but equal

fist—

13.1

(Military Government: General)

When Nellie and Big Bill

sailed from Manila

after four years of entertaining

and nation-building as military governor

and hostess of Malacañang Palace

they brought souvenirs of the East:

carabao hides. Handwoven mats.

Shells, drapes, embroideries.

The Oval Office and High Court

awaited, soon to be

bespangled with island possessions:

scaffold, blindfold, and waterboard.

1.3

(Introduction: Psychology)

Begin with the visible

and the not readily visible

the inexact science of race

apply phrenology

apply hierarchies

be cognizant of the contours of the skull

if the people are difficult to govern

turn

to ecclesiastical power

in each friar a king has

a captain and an army

o

If the native priests are priestesses

or queer / the borders

of woman and man / call them

witches

      rechristen the *babaylan*

as *bruha*—vampires /

aswang who prey

on the pregnant

the weak and infirm

o

Fear is easy to understand
              so Lansdale's men

snatch insurgents and
              slit their throats

hang them up
              -side down to bleed out

then discard the drained
              corpses on the trail

in this manner
              the CIA plant rumors

of aswang among
              the peasants, defanging

the Huk Rebellion
              a species of killing

called *psyops.*

o

The babaylan foresees the

Americans perfecting empire

and counterinsurgency on Leyte

before applying the lessons to Panama

Cuba Santo Domingo Mexico

then Cuba again she suffers

premonitions of Haiti

and Honduras Banana Wars

Border Wars a rush

of bluejackets into Nicaragua

they will call this archipelago the First

Vietnam from the pyre she sings

the future a future of small

wars and occupied countries

TWO-MAN FLOAT, USING PONCHO

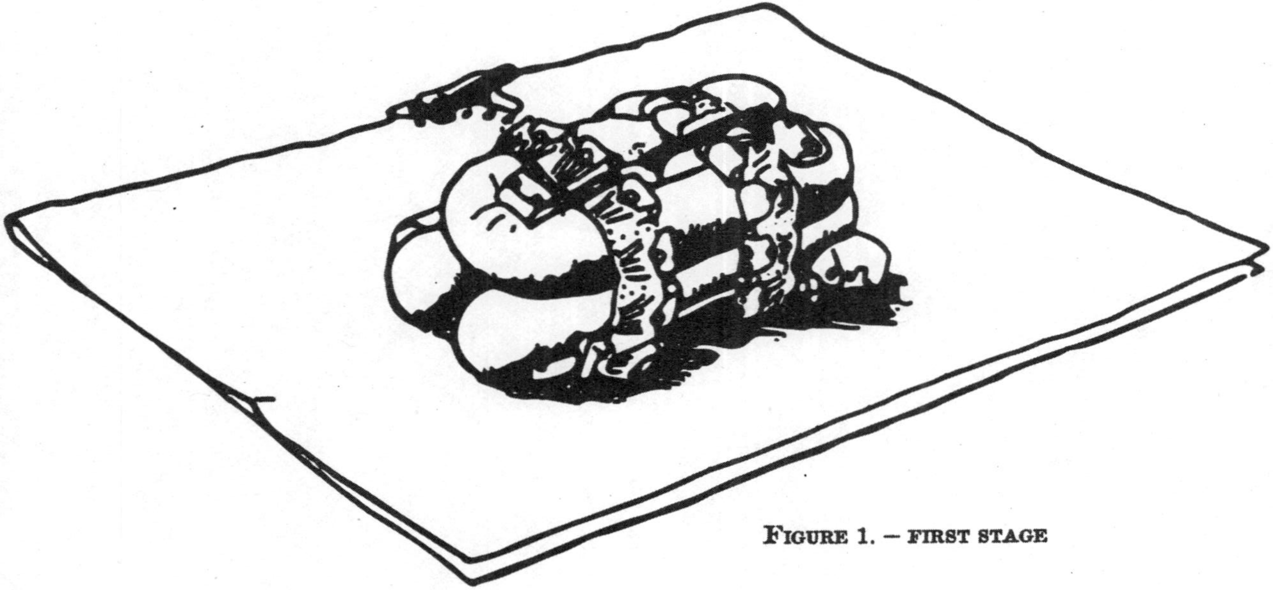

FIGURE 1. — FIRST STAGE

Salvages

Colored troops are to be sent to the Philippines. The sooner the better. The Negroes must be taught that the enemy of the country is a common enemy and that the color of the face has nothing to do with it.
 —*Indianapolis Freeman*, July 1, 1899

The Pasig River, 1899, 5° north of Metro Manila.

I don't know much about dogs but the river
I think is a strong brown dog—rabid, lean & nameless,
a contagion confronting the corps of engineers
in May or what passes for May
swollen with monsoon. So we take
our first casualties, overrun, our ferry
compromised with no shots
fired.   Some
cling to their arms
which sink treacherously as if desperate to hash
at least one kill
& others go bare-handed:
no rail. No chunk of keel.
Gone down
like sailors into Superior
never to rise.
                    Indians we killed killed us
face down
so our souls wouldn't come back;
gators
take you by the wrist. Gators
jaw & roll
so if you wrest free or drift off

(because your bone's bit through)
you won't know which way
is up. You swim deeper
down into the tumid surge, dog
water, choleric muck.
Deeper
looking for refuge—

Infix

What happens when *fantastic*
becomes *fan-fucking-tastic*
was not something I considered
until I tried to learn Tagalog,
the f-bomb in this case an infix,
element that sounds vaguely criminal
but is old as *fuck* itself.
Motherfucker on the other hand's
much younger—*you low-down mother-*
fuckers Sidney Wilson wrote to
the Tennessee Draft Board in 1918
can put a gun in our hands
but who can take it out? Black soldiers
like Pvt. Wilson fought in the Philippines
twenty years earlier & before that saved
Roosevelt's skin at San Juan Hill.
Before the Spaniards they fought Indians:
Kiowa. Comanche: whose children were forced
to forget Nūmū Tekwapū—the Comanche
for Comanche—in English-only schools.
Tagalog agglutinates. Stems
glom tense & tone
like coconut flakes on rice balls.
Kain / *eat* becomes kumain / *will eat*
by subsuming *um* (in English a sound
of uncertainty). Mamatay / *perish*
fibrillates to mamamatay—
one day *you will die.*
The infix marks the shift: *ma,*
as though to go from death
the infinitive to death as future tense
one need only bury their mother.

47

Boondock Suite

boondock—from Tagalog: rough, remote, or isolated country

1

out of sticks   out of storm surge
blockhouse & beachhead

hinterland   backwater   Far
East & wilds

brought back & mis-
pronounced like a war bride

by boys who set out to fight Spain
but became Spain instead:

scour &
scorch the boondocks

looking for *ladrones*

2

Bundok means mountains—peaks, cordilleras.

Best terrain for insurgents to fall back,
splinter off; regroup for new tactics.

                                    For the regulars, a slog.
A sentence: to be picked off by flood
                        fever   ambuscade—

3

Summiting,   they spy *insurrectos*
drilling
in squares far below.

By the time they wind down they
can find only farmers,

            crones, old-timers
& their inscrutable

gugu grins.

4

The Americans' scouts, natives too, shake their heads.
Spit *bundok* as if to explain.

Soft-footed trackers
paid to ferret out   pin down   pour

down throats they pull open
ask questions   pour deeper

5

a man is thrown down on his back & three or four hold him down & a gun
or a rifle or a carbine barrel or stick is thrust in his jaws & his jaws
are thrust back & the water is poured onto his face down his throat
     & nose from a jar
& that is kept up until the man gives some sign or becomes

unconscious

6

Theodore Roosevelt: An old Filipino method of mild torture. Nobody
                              was seriously damaged
                              whereas the

Filipinos had inflicted incredible tortures on our people.

7

        (*water board* née

                           water cure)

8

A soldier who was with General Funston helped to administer the water
cure to 160 natives, all but 26 of whom died:

What kind of water was generally used?
Dirty water was preferred to clean.

Why was that done?
To make the punishment more severe.

9

his sufferings must be that of a man who is drowning

but cannot drown

10

Dear Yusef,

The landscape goes where we go.

It's portable you said   /   veteran
of a later Southeast Asian war.

A reporter.   *Report* as in
to bring back, to carry:

portable.

As in: I carry the Midwest inside me
like a field in which a woman has fallen down

the counties rippling outward
like the opposite of a blast radius

or its homograph. A blast
you said was inside Wood, inside Bird

& Tony Morrison
Willa Cather, Prince & Miles.

In your Bogalusa baritone
                    portable becomes *potable.*

11

Both have to do with barrels

             cupped hands
             canteens
             jugs:

They sent scouts to brim them
             to a typhoidal stew.

                   As though baptism was for
the river's sake & not the sinner's

risen
from lungburst

risen
from gullet to drip

with renewed
                indifference.

12

The water did not cure troop movements
The water did not cure the disfigured
the uprooted the water
did not cure asymmetrically
did not leave a single finger-
print of smoke

the water did not cure the wet open gouge of the water
buffalo half-rising gape-mawed
out of the stream nor did it cure
the bronze-skinned boys blind-
folded mere feet from the muzzles the
water did not   /   /   /   cure

the dust between their toes now
splayed in the dirt not their thirst crowded together and re-

stored to its state before manifest
before destiny
                    agon   archaea

drip of boondock

becoming backwater

Insurrecto

for David Fagen
Corporal, U.S. Army (1898-1899); Captain, Philippine Republican Army
(1899-1901)

Our worst enemy is General May:
rainy season, the lieutenant means, monsoon
much like Tampa's summer storms. Roads become marsh;
not just flooding but fever, a fire
that hollows me out. We throw lifelines
to overturned ferries; casualties grow long.

Incessant drizzle. Letters take too long
to reach home. I prefer carousal, cards: dismay
in officers' faces when I cross the line.
The guardhouse my second home. My fines soon
add up: a month's pay. Most of it earned, so far,
by killing time, not *ladrones*: we march

to summits, spy gugus drilling below; march
back down to find the enemy long
gone—only grinning farmers left. *Hellfire*
spits the lieutenant, scanning ridges, amazed
to have been rolled by shoeless bandits again. Soon
he'll snap, like the officers in Samar who lined

up boys young as ten—sympathizers, aligned
with insurgents. (So said General Smith.) Marshaled
them, blindfolded, to clearings. Too soon
for them to swell the soil; long
rest for short lives. Their will bewilders me—
faced with Gatlings, Krags, methodical shellfire

they ambush hand to hand. Bolos; sniper fire
in enfilades. Harass our lines
then beat back to boondocks, a maze
of jungle, cordilleras, rice fields, marsh.
Land surely rich with poetry—*tulang*
in their tongue—land like home: typhoon

cousin to hurricane. When the monsoon
shifts, so do I—I snap, desert for foreign fires.
Rope can kill black soldiers but not disease, lungs
like ours grittier, the C.O.s say; we're maligned
but nicknamed "Immunes." My old unit marches,
black against brown, under white, as if to make

the Far East a second South. I form a line
alongside former foes, a turncoat merging
nations. Our flag has no color. Soon it may.

TWO-MAN FLOAT, USING PONCHO

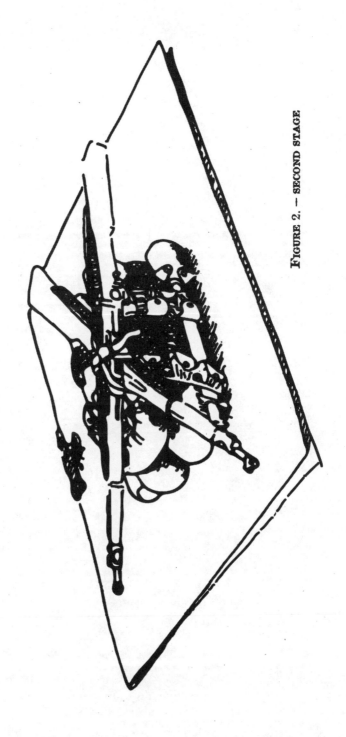

FIGURE 2. — SECOND STAGE

6.4

(Infantry Patrols: Feeding the personnel)

The cure for melancholy is a good tussle.

The cure for a rattlesnake bite
                              is a bell in an unfamiliar country.

Doubt must be carried, aggression replenished.

The cure for democracy is feelings.

                              The irrational can't be treated

by the scientific method;

a man will bleed profusely
                              if pricked by an idea.

The forest will bleed with him.

1.6

(Introduction: Military civil relationship)

A temporary language

should be devised

a pidgin containing

elements of animus

and insubordination

a foreign music

fused with local sound.

If language is a dialect

with an army and a navy

then a pidgin is a turncoat

leading a cadre of guerrillas.

Armed with stolen Mausers

and bolo knives their only

common tongue

is damage.

3.3

(Logistics: Transportation)

Distance to a camel

is but one form

of memory

like the weight of aviaries

dead lakes

cities without roads . . .

Distance

to the mule is work;

for the horse

it's a kind of detachment.

Bulls use distance

to careen and lash.

For a gun it is an instant;

for the spider

crude conversion.

To a tree it's a system

of thought

approaching language.

6.7

(Infantry Patrols: Laying ambushes)

A hush

falls across the trail

deep as a well—

the *ladrones* leave

no footprints; only

night. We remain

motionless, outlines

of light, faces wide open

as if to say *serenade,*

serenade—such falling

among friends—

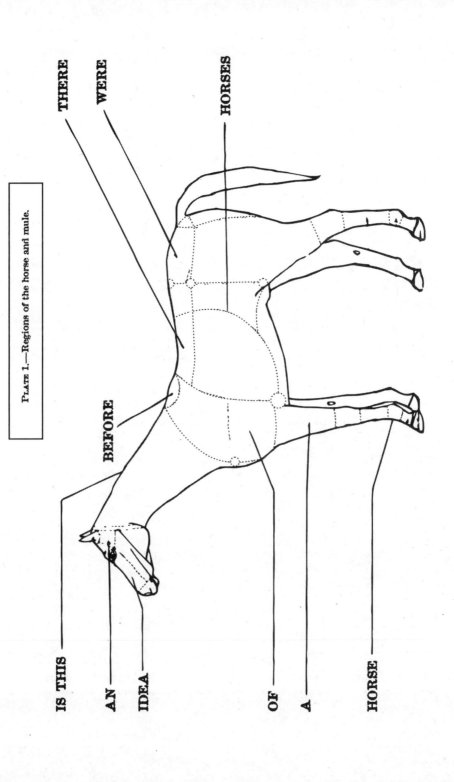

THERE

WERE

HORSES

IS THIS

AN

IDEA

BEFORE

OF

A

HORSE

PLATE 1.—Regions of the horse and mule.

Hitler Moves East

a pecha kucha after David Levinthal & Garry Trudeau

[table]

One takes pictures

the other takes soldiers
& pins them to the mound.

1/32 scale:
grass seed

for wheat fields, Gold
Medal flour for snow.

Trudeau adds gunpowder
like an eight-year-old

salting fries; Levinthal
lights the match—

[explosion]

Boom.
      Soldiers fly back
but don't hit the ground.

It's art
but it's also Sid from *Toy Story*—

boys stringing bombs
to playthings

just to see the legs blown off. *Men*

deal with life William Cowper said
as children with their play

who first misuse / then cast
their toys away.

[field]

The scale makes it easier
to see the infant

in *infantry*. To fall back
to Old French

& further: see *infant*—
the one "unable to speak."

Ditto the dead.

Ditto grunts & snags
church bells melted

for cannons, tin
soldiers blazed up for shot.

[mortar]

Compared to war Patton said
all human endeavor
shrinks to insignificance.

The mortarmen
are the opposite—toys
lensed to light, becoming paper,

then memory.
                The dead
are called into a room
that we can almost enter.

[Operation Barbarossa]

Ukraine.

June 1941: the Germans
sweep east

into an endless country
along a two-thousand mile front.

But Moscow's a camera trick,
always receding.

Winter circles
having caught the scent.

Levinthal tears open
the flour.

[machine gun nest]

To play war, my brother and I
got down in the pile

lined up troops so small
they fit in the curl of my knuckle.

Positioned them in outposts
trenches carved out of

plastic snowpack and in the shadows

of armchairs. Tipping one over
meant notching a kill.

[snowy grave]

Each playset came with a handful
of die-cast troops—

doomed Rebels; Imperials in white
winter hoods—but we

cut out the proofs of purchase
& mailed them in. BUILD

YOUR ARMIES the catalogue said.
The reinforcements arrived

in packets. Like ammo;
like seeds.

[Stahlhelm]

Before drafting for Boeing, Ralph McQuarrie
survived Korea & a shot to the head.
His sketches for Darth Vader
were influenced by kabuto:
samurai headgear.
John Mollo took the sketches
& modeled Vader's helmet
after the Stahlhelm—

the curve of the dome, the flare
of the neck guard.

                      [sidecar]

                  The helmet tells you he
                  is the enemy: the dead-eyed

                  motorcyclist &
                  his sidecar companion.

                  But according to the wizards
                  of Emeryville, California,

                  everything has a soul: not just toys
                  but robots; emotions. Even souls

                  have souls.
                  Even the enemy.

[tank]

Between *Empire* and *Jedi*
we biked to the hobby shop.

Flipped through RPG manuals,
maps, figurines.

I avoided the aisle
of WWII kits—Messerschmitts

with gondola cannons,
tank-busting Sturmoviks—

because it felt like the curtained-off
backroom of Shinders,

the look and smell
of the men who went in.

[wreckage]

Beneath the Airfix box art
depicting a Panzer IV 413

were plastic parts racked to a sprue.
Like a schematic—

the barrel, the turret, the treads.
Once, my brother

shot an oriole with a BB gun.
I was the one

who'd spotted it, bright
as a lure on the power line.

[Messerschmitt]

He was as surprised as I was
when the pellet pierced its skull.

                        The oriole fell
just like a plaything into grass

already gone to seed.
Orioles mate for life

I said as we buried it like a time capsule,
but I was thinking of swans.

[bridge]

Later I built a bridge
out of tongue depressors

wide enough
for an armored column to cross

if it was 1/35 scale
and if there'd been anywhere to go.

At night the silence
of the empty classroom crests

like the silence left by a church bell
after it's taken down

& sent to the ironworks.

[lens flare]

My sons war online.

Their uncle still collects toys

but lately he's been capturing

their souls. There are others

like him—armed with digital

SLRs & online portfolios

of comic book heroes posed as grave

as confederate statues

and gift shop saints.

[wounded]

He can print missing limbs
with his Mars 2 Pro

or parts for swapped
& salvaged fighters:

wing pylons, S-foils.
Sometimes the plastic

comes out stringy like honey
or gut. Sometimes

he twists off pieces & discards
the leftover piping, the joints.

[depot]

PLA filament, derived
from corn starch & sugar cane,
dissolves in a matter
of months.

In temperate climates,
a commissioned officer takes several
years to break down to bones.

Dead passerines
disappear in a handful
of days.

Landfilled army men
green & made of acetate polymers
can last five hundred years.

[soldier]

Five hundred years ago, Crimeans
expelled the Golden Horde.

Five hundred years before that, Pope
Adrian IV crowned Hitler's favorite

Holy Roman Emperor, the red-
bearded Frederick I,

after whom the invasion of Ukraine
was named: Barbarossa.

[cargo hold]

After Mom dies, we clean out the house.

Our aunts divide up the purses & shoes.

Sean rifles through basement boxes of

toys. But there's no sign

of our die-cast troops, so small

they've sunk to the bottoms of bins

& returned to their mineral

origins: aluminum. Copper. Zinc.

[rifle]

All human endeavor shrinks
but even small words

contain worlds. See *seed*.

Sounds in old forms
like *said*.

To paint them my brother must be
steady as a watchmaker,

match the new leg to the torso
like a driver's-side door.

If I wanted to he jokes
I could print the components

for a working gun.
Cede.

[ars poetica]

Anything can fit

in an image: consider

landfill. Consider North

Pacific Gyre. Consider debris fields

floating

in geosynchronous orbit.

How terrible if everything has

a soul—how much more

to answer for; even small wars waged

on the living room floor.

SUPPLY

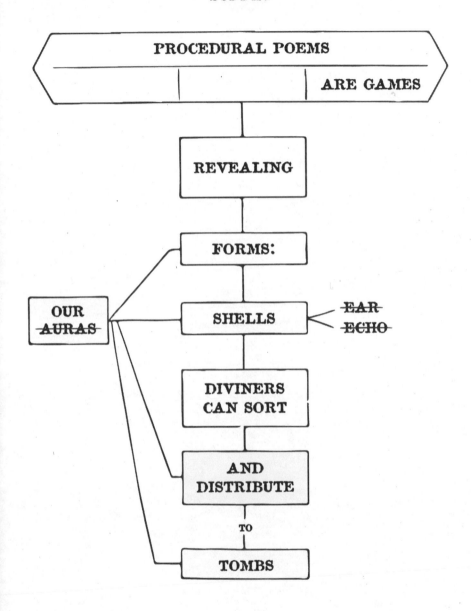

11.1

(Disarmament of Population)

It is customary for a child to possess
miniature weapons and ammunition.

I collected stamps, too, and seashells,
including cowrie shells from the Philippines—

currency for a thousand years
but now game pieces. In *sungka*,

a cousin of mancala, cowrie shells
are placed on a wooden board

shaped like a boat. Shells that land
in empty pits are "dead."

Sungka is a two-player game;
played alone it's a form of divination.

It was when we went back
for my grandfather's funeral

to cities that were never my cities
that I started my collection. Seven

years before he was born there was
a war; that war became a map

and the map became a manual.
I wanted to erase it, not to undo

the past but because the past is still
capable of killing us. Once,

I was taking the Jubilee line
when the train suddenly slowed to a stop.

I made my way to the surface:
London was stopped

in every direction. Someone had found
an unexploded German shell

and it had to be disposed of.
In this variant, the speaker

is a medium and the reader
is a sapper. We are playing

a game; we are disposing
of unexploded ordnance.

7.4

(Mounted Detachments: Mounted detachments)

Don't pack with us.

It's a Filipino joke
a play on accent
f-p substitutions.

We are the best
packers in the world.

We'll pack anything
that moves.
                    It's a form

of first language
interference (*first*

language becomes
pierced language):

we can pack like
animals. If you prefer

you can go and pack
yourself. Because puns

pack meaning, pack
with hierarchies,

pack up borders.
Our motto here is

if you pack with us
we'll pack with you.

after Rex Navarrete & Sarita See

6.8

(Infantry Patrols: Attacking ambushes)

6-75. **Mental preparation.**—**The** principal objective of an offensive ambush is to take advantage of surprise. The closeness and suddenness of the attack is supposed to disorganize and demoralize the enemy. A necessary protection against complete disorganization, and possible demoralization, is to prepare the troops mentally for the shock of ambush. They must be **steel**ed to withstand a sudden blast of fire

came from a jeep

the Americans abandoned after

World War II the leaf spring forge-
welded to
)

h. The *bolo* attack.—In certain theaters of small wars operations there is the possibility that a patrol may be ambushed and rushed from both sides of **the** trail by an enemy armed only with **blade**d weapons. Such attacks are launched from positions located a few feet from the sides of the trail. The use of rifle fire in the general melee which results is fully as dangerous to friendly personnel as to the enemy. The experience of regular forces which have encountered such tactics in the past has indicated that the bayonet is the most satisfactory weapon to combat an attack of this nature.

wide and wickedly curved
a weapon for close combat

knife versus gun
requiring nerve but also

desperation

ORGANIZATION OF A CONSTABULARY

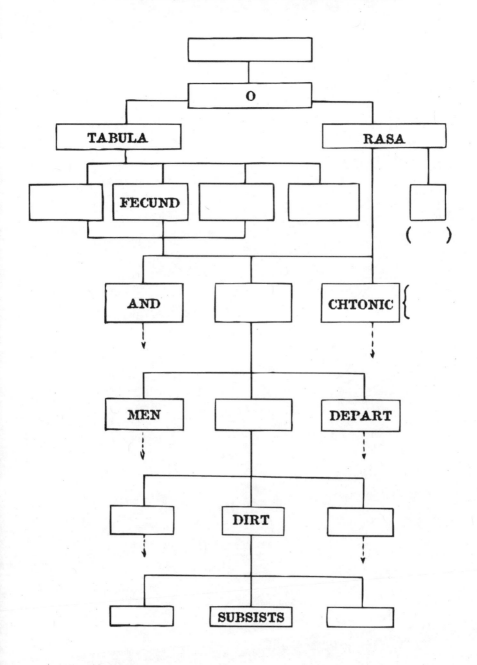

Small Wars

a pecha kucha after An–My Lê

1. Việt Nam.

> I am interested in the Vietnam of the mind.
> —An-My Lê

[Untitled, Thanh Hóa, 1998]

A broad bend of the Mã River.

We approach from above

as if to strafe

but there's no ripple

no fear   only figures

blurred

by leisure & the shutter's

slow sundering

of light

[Untitled, Nam Ha, 1994]

the girl

is a rhyme

so is the helmet   the blouse

spattered with

mud
                    history

has a geologic thickness

but not war   war

is waged with the thin-

nest part of consciousness

[Untitled, Ba Vì, 1998]

I am triggered

by *foreground*   I picture

landscape but where

are the bodies

not beyond the frame

but in the footfalls

an offscreen voice

is called an *acousmêtre*

an offscreen body isn't

even a ghost

[Untitled, Ho Chi Minh City, 1998]

the horizon drops

so low the shutter

can't sharp the barrel-

roll of shade-wings dive-

bombing the crowds fuzzed

by dust as though by rotor

downwash *mors ab*

alto even the girl

gripping a string

[Untitled, Sapa, 1995]

any child

can tell you the opposite

of fire but what is

the opposite of napalm

the pail he carries gets

heavier the closer he gets to

the lens the bellows a well

of gravity a concertinaed

son *too hot* he is not

any child *too hot*

he is ours

[Untitled, Hanoi, 1998]

the kind of room

they took my uncle to in

Camp Crame Manila 1973

the chair & foldout table   window

fogged with houses   would you care

for a cigarette   the century

has been kind—we have

all the time in the world

[Untitled, Ho Chi Minh City, 1995]

as if to flee by boat

toward a shore of unlit neon

Compaq   Carlsberg

Panasonic Diamond-

Shamrock   orange is

colorless *chất độc màu*

da cam even in the color-

blind pages called *Time*

2. Small Wars.

All wars are fought twice, the first time on the battlefield, the second time in memory.
—Viet Nguyen

[Sniper I, 1999–2002]

This sentence is

a simulation (what sentence

is not)   there are men in it motion-

blurred except

for the eyes there

is black hair black–

sleeves lining up if we look

through the eyes of the photographer

whose eyes

does she look through

[Tall Grass II, 1999–2002]

if the landscape is a character

what is its arc

who played it last   killed

in the first act what comes

back in the view-

finder as yellow pine

not fan palm

cedar &

susurrations of tufted

hairgrass

[Rescue, 1999–2002]

say *fuselage*

& the mind

makes wreckage

so smoke to plush the steel

& pencil to mark

parabolae

what if time is to

grammar as herbicide

is to canopy

[Lesson, 1999–2002]

let's you & me war-game this

Nixon to Kissinger 1970

hard at work reading tea

leaves the opposite of

reenacting which makes

the ground a Ouija board

to spell the next question

the photographer plays the

enemy   lets herself be

lensed by her own planchette

[Distant Flare, 1999–2002]

you see now that war is sorcery

I do not mean witches

I mean it is made

in the dark   the ancient

forest   like the first

murder

like the slow rounds

of faeries

a forge   siring

forges

[Bamboo, 1999–2002]

if every war

               is fought twice

which time

is this

      quiet—

                  count

to twenty

3. 29 Palms.

I am more interested in the precursor to war and its psychic aftermath.
    —An-My Lê

[Infantry Officers' Brief, 2003–4]

The California desert.

How are men different

from hills

twenty & huddled like

chaparral stones

         shade

proliferates   & under

this new tissue the fever

comes down

[Infantry Platoon, Alpha Company, 2003–4]

sleeping back-

to-back we rise   white-

hot as static

the camo netting

ten thousand paper

cranes—

in between raids

there is waiting

this in-between

is what we are in now

[Captain Folsom, 2003–4]

you can imagine hitting

the tank from here

with a rock or rocket–

propelled grenade & how

long it would take the punch–

drunk turret to find

a ballistic solution the bush

you're crouched in clear

as kindling the sun

so slow it could take

all afternoon

[Combat Operations Center Guard, 2003–4]

practice watchfulness practice

middle-

distance practice boredom

beside the razor wire coiling

past like the contrail of a good

idea the desert

a simulation just ask

the departed buried

under a crosshair

that grave is either empty

or it's ours

[Explosive Ordinance Disposal, 2003–4]

does it sound like a practice room

inside the bombsuit

is the robot the kind the Dallas

Police rigged with a pound

of C-4 to kill the cop-

killer   when its gripper

opens does it sound like the trap-

door in the anatomical theater

vanishing the cut & unused

Renaissance parts

[Security and Stabilization Operations, Graffiti, 2003–4]

a garland of GOOD SADDAM

fake Arabic FREE

SADDAM like w's left

in the sun like the asses

schoolchildren graffiti

above urinals GO HOME

a colon floats like a free

radical separating

neither seconds nor tenths of

seconds   preceding

no list

[Night Operations III, 2003–4]

if lightning is made

entirely of error what

is an air strike   impossible

to tell who is striking

who the desert or the

night sky

but possible now to imagine

death arriving as

light & light

the cessation of time

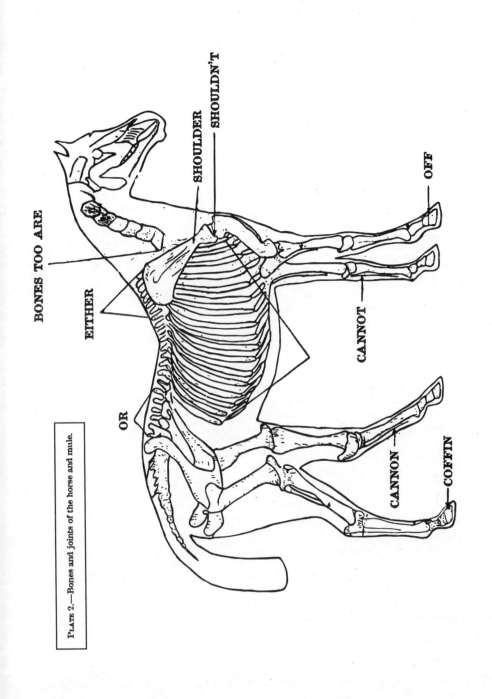

BONES TOO ARE

SHOULDER

SHOULDN'T

EITHER

OR

OFF

CANNOT

CANNON

COFFIN

Plate 2.—Bones and joints of the horse and mule.

6.9

(Infantry Patrols: Attacking houses)

Darkness is hard to control

it makes too much noise

barking at Venus

at churches and their corneas of

fired glass

better to let the lead

fulfill its rapturous purpose

14.3

(Supervision of Elections: Electoral mission)

Choose—polonaise
or nocturne.

Overture or epilogue.
Aubade, lullaby—kundiman

or condemnation.
                              Kundiman means
serenade;

serenade means night,
a window, and

the beloved.
                    And if the beloved

is a nation, if night is
an occupying force

then what is a window
what of the garden

sprawled below—
                              to whom are you
making promises?

6.12

(Infantry Patrols: Special operations)

azimuth: from the Arabic *as-samt:* "The direction; the way."

        Cut a wedge
        out of ground and night sky.
                    Stars
        can guide bayonets

        but also refugees.

6.10

(Infantry Patrols: Stratagems & ruses)

Always dance

with the hostess

plant rumors

& late night rendezvous

cultivate sentimental ruses

scatter violets

on the graves of enemies

PERSONNEL

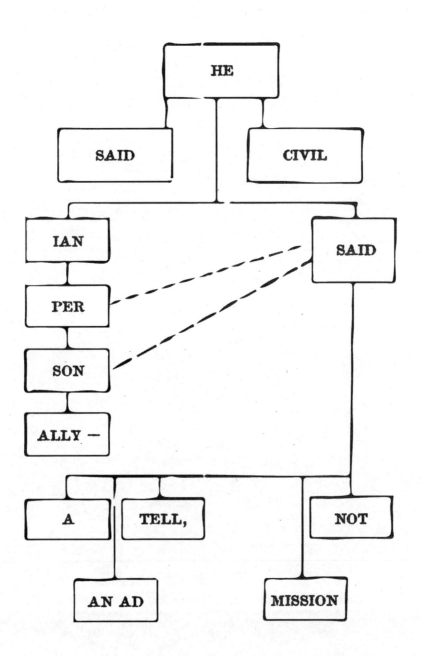

States & Capitals

The capital of January is January.
The capital of a hospital is the morgue.
The capital of the morgue
is a refrigerated truck. The capital of the truck
is oil. Oil tells the President
to stand down. The President looks toward the Capitol
Building. It is a capital
idea. The sentries that guard the idea
do not believe in it. They believe
in the guarding; that only they know
who it must be guarded from. The capital
is in each of them. It is infected
with the anti-idea, the belief
in the President. The viral load
increases. The capital thick
with infection. The virus
builds its capital in each branch
of the lung. When the lungs no longer
work it moves its capital
to the trash-covered ground.
The capital of death
is under siege. Death builds its capital
in America. The nursery
is the capital of Death. Death is a country
lacking hospital beds.
Inside the cab of its refrigerated truck
Death idles the engine.

New Classmate

As though the ocean had joined our kindergarten midyear
& not a refugee.

                    Little English
& a transistor hearing aid

strapped to his chest like an answering machine.

They asked me to sit with him
afternoons
                at the long library table

to work on greetings, colors,
                                shapes.

When we got to black
I pointed at his hair
                & he smiled & pointed at mine.

Static sheared the air: Soon
I realized that if he chuckled

or even grinned
we would both be flooded with feedback.

He smiled anyway
confident of every word, teaching me its confederate

in Vietnamese.
At first I bristled. I didn't need the ocean.

I could ride for hours in any direction & still be surrounded by hills;

further & the moonscape of the Badlands;
        keep going & I'm old enough to drive, to idle

the car beside a smattering of bison—
                    not extinct after all
but not going anywhere either.

                  Only war
could tuck the sea into a boat

& shipwreck it on shag,
              in supermarkets, could force it
to come to grips with plow schedules,

the workings of a gas range.
              Who was I
but another brown child

        a name that had to be pronounced
twice? What I remember isn't our words

but a range of possible meanings—red
to red again.

Golden Age

It used to embarrass me when my father talked
back to the TV.

Since my mother died he doesn't talk anymore
but falls asleep enwombed

by voices: anchors,
procedurals, the invisible labor

of foley artists. My teacher
gasped when the *Challenger*

exploded on live TV. We had to wait
for the set to warm up

from a white hot pinprick of light.
It was so heavy the librarian warned

it could crush us. We watched as the column
of smoke split in two. *Gasp*

comes from Old Norse *geispa*
& shares a base with *brag, bluster,*

& *babble.* My second week of
teaching Kindergarten a girl came in &

said she saw a plane on TV
fly into a tower. By the end of the day

a colleague had rushed in & announced
that we'd started to bomb

Afghanistan.
We are still bombing Afghanistan.

My father turns the volume up
to 77, 78. Each morning I have to crank

the volume back down.
His hearing loss could be described

as severe to profound. Still he must feel
bathed in those shifting backdrops,

those faces, *profound* from the Latin for before
the bottom. In order to remember

what to capitalize in *McAuliffe*
I think of how it contains the chemical

symbol for gold. The noise
of the television soothes everyone

on the other side of the house; it tells us
someone is watching but not watching

us, not the room where we can finally
make love undetected. I was taught to be silent

when praying. She was taught to pray
out loud, the way our sons

threw up their hands when we could solve
any unhappiness by lifting them: *up*

they would say. Up. The crew
of the *Challenger* were likely conscious

the whole way down.   I want
to lay like this a little longer,

before getting up, before
erasing all traces

of intimacy. Sometimes I go back out
& pour my father a finger of Jura

& he pretends he hasn't been sleeping.
I've been doing this since I was a boy,

sneaking out after bedtime & over
my father's shoulder watching the cold

war unfold. The atomic
number for gold is 79. *God*

he says when there's a protest,
a wildfire, a shooting.

God as though
there were someone else in the room.

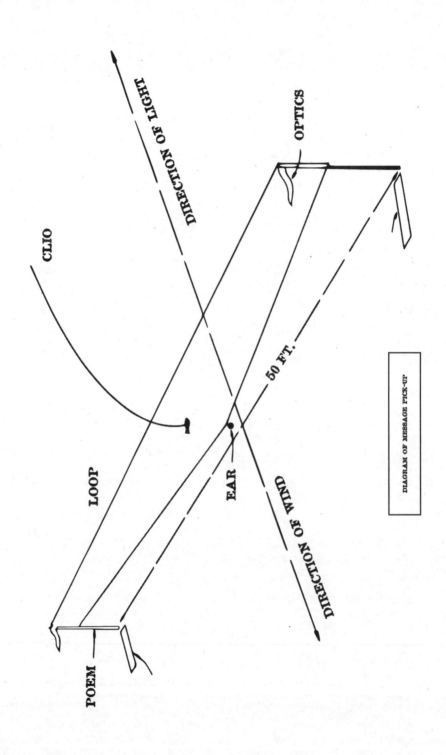

CLIO

DIRECTION OF LIGHT

OPTICS

LOOP

POEM

EAR

50 FT.

DIRECTION OF WIND

DIAGRAM OF MESSAGE PICK-UP

3.2

(Logistics: Supply)

It is desirable to the Mindanao bleeding-heart
not to be found

especially in the rainy season.

                             Consider
the white chin and throat
and against all tropical reason

the pistol-wound patch
on her chest—

woo–oo
woo–oo

indistinguishable from a common pigeon
or dove.

There's a myth about the Nazarene:
After the Roman pierced

his side a dove
brushed against the wound.

That the dove's descendants
are stained makes this a story about

the accumulation of trauma.

9

(Aviation)

(I)

the aviator

must know the ground

the way the light

knows the retina

(II)

the image

a nose dive

a kind of crash—

object permanence

keeps

the plane in the air

(III)

but the drone operator

seldom leaves

the ground

beyond the barbed wire is

the Cold Creek range

Indian Springs dusty and

remote and Irish

Car Bomb

the barrelhouse special

(IV)

each flight disrupts

the attention

of the ground

(V)

a Predator drone

can pick targets on its own

after it culls and data-

mines terabytes of

surveillance images

in computing

object persistence means

that even after a cause has been removed

the data survives

(VI)

ganglion cells in

the retinas of the blind

register light

a signal is sent

to the brain

but isn't converted to sight

(VII)

a drone pilot might

observe a target for months

might watch him grieve

cheat and practice

penalties with his kids

then one day when

the conditions have all been

met you kill him

you watch the death

you even follow the body

to the burial ground

and kill the gathered mourners

6.1

(Infantry Patrols: Small war tactics)

Most of the body
is rain

is it raining
on the cities and towns

on the Pacific
and the defenseless here-

after——. It was
evening all day

thunder
strafed the roofs

of churches
and hothouses——

15

(Withdrawal)

(I)

expect withdrawal

symptoms expect

anxiety   depression

the inability to fire

and forget

(II)

when the outlying districts

smolder

when the crowds crush

the barbed wire the airfield the crowds

when evacuees cleave

to wing and wheel-

well we fall

in supplication

(III)

a surge is an open secret

so is a drawdown .

o

a fragment of a fragment

can still be lethal

o

                isn't the body

                a cargo hold crammed with

                the dead and the chance

                for continuity

o

a C-17 can airlift over-

sized payloads medical

supplies presidential

motorcades even eight

hundred refugees shoulder

to shoulder a waiting room

packed with names

that may never be called

14.1

(Supervision of Elections: General)

If the President of the United States overturns

an election if he overturns majority rule

if the President of the United States

overturns a teacup a hurricane if he

overturns Mexico and the division

of present from past if he railroads

a virus through the House if

the police cannot be depended upon

and the golden rule is rescinded

by executive order then the manual

is not a manual but a map found

in an attic the continents too

large too close or missing entirely

the shorelines garbled and

beset by serpents

4.5

(Training: Training programs and schedules)

The too-long-

didn't-read version:

peacetime

is the training period

war is the performance.

My children

have never seen war.

It is also true

that they have never lived

without it.

1.5

(Introduction: The chain of command)

on the shores of an un-

familiar country

trust the impulse

for analogy

each

          to   each

and else to elsewhere

to call the world an ocean is

an error

          the world

is an island

and you are half ship-

wreck half siren

5.2

(Initial Operations: Movement inland)

5-7. **Point of departure.**—a. As in all forms of warfare, logistic requirements must be given careful consideration in preparing strategies and tactical plans; in fact such requirements are frequently the determining factor. Before a movement inland is undertaken an analysis and estimate of the local transportation and supply facilities must be made in order to insure a reasonable rate of advance with replacement of supplies.

b. The movement inland will not always be a movement from a seaport to the interior. Frequently the movement will be made from the capital or principal city, located at the terminus of a railroad at the head of navigation on the upper part of a large river, or on a well-developed highway, with well-defined lines of communication connecting it with the seacoast. In any case the point of departure becomes a base of operations as well as a base of supply until other bases more advanced are established. Should the small-war operations be initiated by the establishment of neutral zones, one or more of them may later become a base for extended operations.

c. If the point of departure for the movement inland is to be other than a seaport, the movement to the point is made by the most convenient means. The movement will be of the same general nature as an advance in major warfare in the presence of the enemy. The special features of a movement by **inland** waterways **are** presented in chapter XII.

5-8. **Mobile flying columns.**—a. When the successful prosecution of the campaign requires the execution of measures beyond and/or supplementary to the establishment of neutral zones, the control of seaports, or key **cities** along the lines **of** communication in the affected areas, mobile columns must be projected inland from the point of

Inland are cities of light

sprawling machines

that can traverse the past.

By means of light, one can

touch the beginning of

time itself: It is a column

of fire, impenetrable, bent

to the body like an opera

containing the sea,

the rolling sea minus

the gondolas. The engine

is made of singing.

Notes

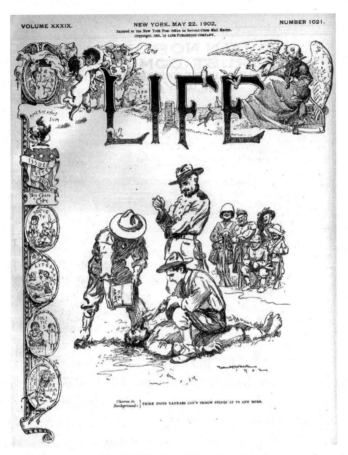

Cover of *Life* magazine by W. Watkins, May 22, 1902, depicting American soldiers subjecting a Filipino prisoner to the "Water Cure."

2.1 — "Note: The poems with numbered titles": The United States Marine Corps *Small Wars Manual* (1940) is considered a classic of military science, gathering together the experiences, analyses, and insights gained by waging guerilla wars and military inventions from the 1890s to the 1930s in Cuba, the Philippines, Panama, Honduras, Nicaragua, the Dominican Republic, Haiti, and Mexico. Major General James Mattis, who would later serve as Secretary of Defense in the Trump Administration, included the *SWM* in his required reading lists for officers serving in Iraq and Afghanistan.

14.5 — *"The president from Canton":* The Temple of Music was an auditorium built for the Pan-American Exposition in Buffalo, New York, and was the site of the 1901 assassination of President William McKinley.

1.1 — *"A 'small war' / is a state of exception":* For more on the Oval Office under William Howard Taft and President Taft's inclusion of mementos from his service as governor-general of the Philippines, see David Brody's *Visualizing American Empire: Orientalism and Imperialism in the Philippines*.

4.3 — *"Eighteen ninety-nine. / A colored private":* "In late 1899," the historian Noel Jacob Kent writes in *America in 1900*, "fighting broke out between black and white soldiers on transport ships carrying them to the Philippines."

13.1 — *"When Nellie and Big Bill / sailed from Manila":* The term *waterboarding* did not enter the public discourse until 2004, but historians such as Paul Kramer and Ed Peters have noted the similarities between the waterboarding of detainees after 9/11 and the use of the so-called *water cure* during the Philippine-American War. During congressional hearings, Taft admitted that American soldiers had administered the water cure to Filipinos. Taft is the only person to have served as both POTUS and chief justice of the Supreme Court.

1.3 — *"Begin with the visible":* I'm indebted to Caroline Brewer's *Shamanism, Catholicism, and Gender Relations in Colonial Philippines, 1521-1685*, for shedding light on how the babaylan—indigenous shamans who were predominantly women or gender nonconforming men—and their spiritual practices were suppressed and demonized by their Catholic colonizers, leading to the myth of the aswang, a vampire-like creature that preys on pregnant women.

Edward Lansdale developed the use of psychological warfare (psyops) as part of the CIA's efforts to suppress communist insurgencies in the Philippines (the Hukbalahap or "Huk" Rebellion) and in Vietnam. For a compelling account of the Huk Rebellion told from the point of view of the partisans, see Carlos Bulosan's unfinished novel *The Cry and the Dedication*.

"Infix": The quotation from Sidney Wilson (from *Letter* in *Journal of American History*, 1995, vol. 81) was cited in the *Oxford English Dictionary* as one of the earliest uses of this expletive.

"Boondock Suite": The poem quotes and paraphrases from multiple sources, including: *The Letters of Theodore Roosevelt*; "One 'Water Cure' Victim: Witness Tells of the Case Before the Senate Committee," *The New York Times*, May 11, 1902; Moorfield Storey & Julian Codman's *Secretary Root's Record: "Marked Severities" in Philippine Warfare*; Stuart Creighton Miller, *"Benevolent Assimilation": The American Conquest of the Philippines, 1899-1903*; and talks given by Yusef Komunyakaa at the William Joiner Institute for the Study of War and Social Consequences in 1997 and at the University of Southern California in 2014.

"Insurrecto": For further reading on David Fagen, see Michael Morey's *Fagen: An African American Renegade in the Philippine-American War*.

For their scholarship and insights into the all-Black regiments who served in the Philippine-American War, I am indebted to Cynthia Marasigan and to Willard P. Gatewood, Jr., particularly Gatewood's *Smoked Yankees and the Struggle for Empire: Letters from Negro Soldiers 1898-1902* and *Black Americans and the White Man's Burden, 1898-1903*.

In response to the fifty-four American soldiers killed in a surprise attack in the town of Balangiga, Brigadier General Jacob H. Smith ordered the execution of all Filipino males over the age of ten, saying, "I want no prisoners. I wish you to kill and burn, the more you kill and burn the better it will please me." Smith was tried for his conduct but received no punishment other than forced early retirement.

"Kill everyone over ten," a political cartoon by Homer Davenport, was originally published in the *New York Journal* on May 5, 1902.

During the Spanish-American and Philippine-American Wars, policy-makers operated under the racist assumption that Black soldiers were immune to tropical diseases. Consequently, troops who had earned the sobriquet "Buffalo Soldiers" in the American West also came to be known as the "Immune" regiments.

1.6 — "A temporary language / should be devised": "A language is a dialect with an army and a navy" is a saying popularized by linguist and Yiddish scholar Max Weinreich, who expressed it in Yiddish: "מיט אן ארמיי און פֿלאָט
אַ שפּראַך איז אַ דיאלעקט"

"Plate 1—Regions of the horse and mule" borrows a fragment from the title poem of Yusef Komunyakaa's *War Horses*.

"Hitler Moves East" — David Levinthal and Garry Trudeau created *Hitler Moves East*—what the two friends describe as a "paper movie"—as graduate students at Yale University in 1975, using cheap, plastic toy soldiers and model tanks. The resulting sepia-toned images, which played with the conventions of photojournalism, were published as a book in 1977 and established Levinthal's toy-centric practice of photography. The untitled photograph used on the cover of this book serves as the inspiration for the section titled "[mortar]."

7.4 — "Don't pack with us": In comedian Rex Navarrette's skit "SBC Packers," Filipino immigrants repeatedly muddle the distinction between *f* and *p* sounds, resulting in a string of indecorous double entendres. In Chapter 3 of *The Decolonized Eye* ("Why Filipinos Make Pun(s) of Each Other: *The* Sikolohiya/*Psychology of Rex Navarrette's Stand-up Comedy*"), Sarita See cites Navarrette's jokes as a prime example of the "[p]olemical, aggressive, and frivolous forms of wordplay" that permeate everyday Filipino/American life. These jokes are "evidence of a culture" that is not only "alive and vibrant" but that consciously subverts colonial and neocolonial hierarchies.

"Small Wars": The epigraphs for parts 1 and 3 of *Small Wars* come from Hilton Als's interview with the artist included in *An-My Lê: Small Wars*. The epigraph for part 2 of the pecha kucha comes from Viet Thanh Nguyen's *Nothing Ever Dies: Vietnam and the Memory of War*.

Acousmêtre is a term coined by French film theorist Michel Chion to describe cinematic voices that are heard but not seen.

Mors ab alto, "death from above" in Latin, is the motto for the United States Air Force 7th Bombardment Wing.

"[Night Operations III, 2003–4]" paraphrases a line by Galway Kinnell.

14.3 — "*Choose—polonaise / or nocturne*": During the Spanish colonial period, the *kundiman*, a type of Filipino love song, was often employed by singers and songwriters as a way to express nationalistic sentiment disguised in traditional themes of courtship and thereby avoid censorship.

9 — "*the aviator / must know the ground*": Part VII paraphrases Neal Scheuneman, a retired drone sensor operator and master sergeant from the Air Force, as interviewed in the *New York Times* article, "The Unseen Scars of Those Who Kill Via Remote Control," Dave Philipps, April 15, 2022.

Acknowledgments

Many thanks to the editors of the *Adroit Journal, Beloit Poetry Journal, Conduit, Consequence Magazine, Copper Nickel, Couplet Poetry, Guernica,* and *Mayday,* in which these poems, sometimes in earlier versions, first appeared.

"Insurrecto" was selected by Joseph Legaspi for the Academy of American Poets series *Poem-a-Day.* "Golden Age" was selected by Ada Limón for episode 571 of American Public Media's *The Slowdown.*

Thank you to the McKnight Foundation and to Solmaz Sharif and Bao Phi for the support that made many of these poems possible.

To Daniel Slager and to the wonderful team at Milkweed Editions for your support and for your belief in this project. Thank you to Bailey Hutchinson, Lauren Langston Klein, and Mary Austin Speaker for your meticulous editorial and design work.

To Yuri Takasugi Santiago for her artistry, patience, and graphic design wizardry in "erasing" the SMW's figures and tables.

To Mike Bazzett, who not only helped with individual poems but who helped me find the form.

To Brandon Som, Wayne Miller, Diana Arterian, Cathy Linh Che, Sun Yung Shin, Su Hwang, David Walker, Doug Kearney, Monica Ong Reed, Melissa Gabbert, Keith Wilson, Leslie Adrienne Miller, Todd Lawrence, and Joel Hernandez for their continued friendship, wisdom, and encouragement throughout the making of these poems, and to Srikanth Reddy and Claudia Rankine, for their early feedback and encouragement of this project.

To my teachers who have continued to give me guidance, especially David St. John, Viet Nguyen, and Oliver de la Paz.

To my students, who give me hope and inspiration, to my colleagues at CalArts and at the University of St. Thomas, and to our community in the Twin Cities, Pasadena, and elsewhere, especially to the Santiagos, the Takasugis, and the Vuongs.

And most of all to Yuri, Aki, and Tristan, who are my hope and my reason.

Chris Santiago's debut collection *Tula* was selected by A. Van Jordan as the winner of the Lindquist & Vennum Poetry Prize and was a finalist for the Minnesota Book Award. His poems have appeared in *Poetry Magazine*, *Copper Nickel*, *Conduit*, The Academy of American Poets *Poem-a-Day*, and American Public Media's *The Slowdown*. His collaboration with composer Lembit Beecher and ethnographer Todd Lawrence, *Say Home*, was commissioned by the Saint Paul Chamber Orchestra and received its world premiere at the Ordway in 2019. A Loft Poetry Mentor and Fellow of the McKnight Foundation, the Mellon Foundation/ACLS, Kundiman, and the National Endowment for the Arts, he received his PhD from the University of Southern California and recently joined the Faculty of the School of Critical Studies at CalArts in Santa Clarita, California. He lives in Pasadena.

milkweed
EDITIONS

Founded as a nonprofit organization in 1980, Milkweed Editions is an independent publisher. Our mission is to identify, nurture, and publish transformative literature, and build an engaged community around it.

We are based in Bdé Óta Othúŋwe (Minneapolis) in Mní Sota Makhóčhe (Minnesota), the traditional homeland of the Dakhóta and Anishinaabe (Ojibwe) people and current home to many thousands of Dakhóta, Ojibwe, and other Indigenous people, including four federally recognized Dakhóta nations and seven federally recognized Ojibwe nations.

We believe all flourishing is mutual, and we envision a future in which all can thrive. Realizing such a vision requires reflection on historical legacies and engagement with current realities. We humbly encourage readers to do the same.

milkweed.org

Milkweed Editions, an independent nonprofit literary publisher, gratefully acknowledges sustaining support from our board of directors, the McKnight Foundation, the National Endowment for the Arts, and many generous contributions from foundations, corporations, and thousands of individuals—our readers. This activity is made possible by the voters of Minnesota through a Minnesota State Arts Board Operating Support grant, thanks to a legislative appropriation from the Arts and Cultural Heritage Fund.

Interior design by Tijqua Daiker
Typeset in Adobe Caslon Pro

Adobe Caslon Pro was created by Carol Twombly
for Adobe Systems in 1990. Her design was inspired by
the family of typefaces cut by the celebrated engraver
William Caslon I, whose family foundry served
England with clean, elegant type from the early
Enlightenment through the turn of the
twentieth century.